THE YEAR OF LIVING PERILOUSLY

More Cartoons by Pat Oliphant

Foreword by David Hume Kennerly

Andrews, McMeel & Parker
A Universal Press Syndicate Company
Kansas City ● New York

Foreword

Oliphant finally got smart. He asked a photographer to do the foreword to his book. I suppose after Larry King and Studs Terkel, there really wasn't much room left for a legitimate writer.

My first exposure to Pat Oliphant was at a cocktail party in Washington, D.C. I expressed admiration for his work, and asked him if he knew a few other editorial cartoonists who were friends of mine. He did. How did he like their work? He didn't. It was the beginning of a wonderful relationship.

A few notes on our man Oliphant. He was born Patrick Oliphant in Adelaide, Australia, a long time ago. He started, as you were supposed to in this business, as a copyboy. After probably telling one too many editors what they could do with their copy, he began cartooning.

Shortly thereafter he placed second in the funniest cartoonist contest sponsored by the International Federation of Free Journalists in Fleet Street (making me wonder who could have been funnier!). Being second isn't part of Oliphant's nature — in 1967 he won the Pulitzer Prize for editorial cartooning.

But enough of all that. We want to know about the guy behind the pen. Who is that bespectacled person who runs roughshod over today's political figures? Is he really a cold-hearted son-of-a-bitch, or in fact a sensitive, caring human being? Neither. In fact, he's a sensitive son-of-a-bitch. After a long dinner one evening, shortly after the bombing of the U.S. Marine compound in Beirut, Pat and I were discussing television coverage of the families of the dead or missing marines. We both thought the coverage was a major intrusion into their lives. The next morning Oliphant did something about it. He drew a cartoon showing a pack of jackals carrying TV cameras and microphones charging the front door of a home, "We hear your son may be a casualty in the Beirut bombing. Give us some color on that — like anguish, grief, how do you feel about it. ..."

There is, of course, a quiet Oliphant. In December of 1983 we spent a week together in Jamaica. Oliphant's main activities, which took place in no particular order but with great regularity, included sipping vodka under a big tree as he read a book, sipping vodka as he paddled about in a canoe, reclining in a hammock sipping vodka, or just sipping vodka. His serenity was interrupted only once that week by a loudspeaker truck extolling the virtues of a local politician by the name of Buxton Cook. "Just like home, Mug," he said with a wink. He didn't draw a thing.

He did, however, draw a whole lot before and after. *The Year of Living Perilously* is a collection of that work.

Cheers!

DAVID HUME KENNERLY
Washington, D.C.
May 12, 1984

(Notes on Kennerly: *Started his career on the* Portland Oregonian, *where he was not a copyboy. UPI staff photographer in Los Angeles, New York, Washington, D.C., and Vietnam, where he won the 1972 Pulitzer Prize for feature photography. Returned to D.C. as a photographer for* Time *magazine in 1973, became personal photographer for President Gerald Ford during his administration. Currently living in D.C. working as* Time *photographer. Has twenty* Time *covers, and has travelled in over a hundred countries on assignment. Now he's going off to Hollywood to learn film directing. Who does he think he is? —* Pat Oliphant)

CHIVALRY LIVETH!

British Prime Minister Thatcher visits the U.S. for the Williamsburg Summit Meeting.*

This and all other postscripts by Pat Oliphant.

For the manyeth time, the president proclaims his undying affection for James Watt.

Sally Ride, first U.S. woman in space. Nobody remembers who those other jokers were.

The pope visits Poland. General Jaruzelski is understandably tense. . . .

Ex-V.P. Mondale on the primary trail.

Pioneer 10, bearing semi-explicit pictures of earthlings, passes out of our solar system on a voyage to who-knows-where. . . .

June 27, 1983

Who stole President Carter's briefing book? Who passed it to the Reagan coaching team before the
Carter-Reagan debate? CIA Director Casey claims amnesia.

He doesn't know either. Which figures.

* I remember Walt Kelly, creator of Pogo, as one of the finer people I ever met. He died in 1973. For a touch of the South, this cartoon was drawn in his style.

June 30, 1983

"THE LAW GIVETH AND THE LAW TAKETH AWAY. TUITION TAX CREDITS BE-ETH THE NAME OF THE GAME!"

There are many sides to this question. This has been one of them.

'WHAT LITTLE JAPANESE CARS?'

RONALD REAGAN MEETS ANSEL ADAMS

President Reagan enjoys doing this to photographers. . . . He also enjoys doing this to the environment. . . . No wonder
Ansel came away from their meeting shaking his head.

July 8, 1983

'WELL...WE BALLOONISTS TRADITIONALLY BREAK OUT THE CHAMPAGNE TO TOAST A SUCCESSFUL FLIGHT.'

'WE THANK THEE FOR THE GIFTS OF THY BOUNTIFUL HERPES AND THINE BLESSED AIDS, O, LORD...
NOW SEND US SOMETHING FOR ALL THE OTHER WEIRDOS.'

'WADDAYAKNOW — TAKE A SNIFF AT THIS OLD STUFF AND TELL ME WHAT IT IS... NERVE GAS, RIGHT?'

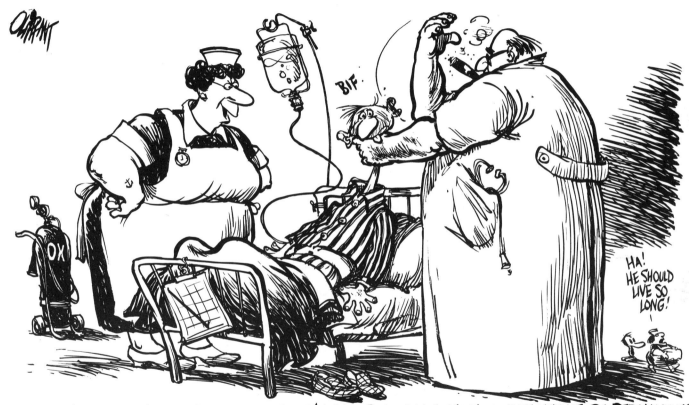

'DR. VOLCKER WANTS YOU TO SLOW DOWN. DR. VOLCKER SAYS HE WANTS YOUR RECOVERY TO BE PERMANENT.'

OK! OK!

'TELL SEYMOUR HERSH DER LONE RANGER'S BACK IN TOWN!'

Seymour Hersh devastates Lone Ranger Kissinger in a new book. Lone Ranger is not amused.

'WELL, GENERAL, THAT LITTLE GIZMO WOULD NORMALLY RUN YOU 85 CENTS. BUT FOR THE U.S. ARMED FORCES, I COULD MARK IT DOWN TO FIVE HUNDRED BUCKS...KNOW WHAT I MEAN?'

July 21, 1983

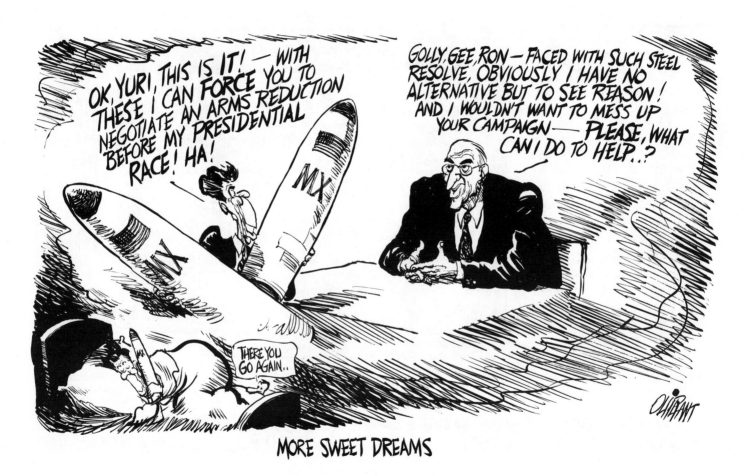

MORE SWEET DREAMS

At the National Zoo, the new baby panda dies.

The Debategate inquiry reveals that columnist George Will acted as a coach during Reagan's debate practice. "Mr. Reagan," trilled Mr. Will, "behaved like a thoroughbred."

The Pentagon claims it doesn't do this anymore.

July 29, 1983

THE SILENCED MAJORITY

Helping others to help themselves — who says he's heartless and uncaring? . . . Well, apart from you . . .

That's what the president said. The president will say anything he thinks you want to hear.
Speak for yourself, Mr. President.

Orphaned by Ma Bell.

Begin says he'll resign.

Begin indeed *does* resign.

CLAWS

Korean civilian airliner shot down by Russians.

After the Korean 747 is shot down, our West European allies rush to impose sanctions against the USSR.

GROMYKO'S APOLOGY

The last word . . .

. . . except for a few words from the gentleman to our right.

Like we said, whatever you want to hear . . .

'MCGOVERN FOR PRESIDENT! STOP THE WAR! BRING THE TROOPS HOME!
GIVE EVERYBODY A FREE THOUSAND BUCKS! WADDAYASAY?...'

McGovern announces for the Democratic primaries. They could have done worse. They DID do worse. . . .

'WELL, IF YOU DON'T WANT OUR HELP, MAYBE YOU COULD TRY CHEWING YOUR LEG OFF, OR SOMETHING.'

'HOWEVER, AND ON THE OTHER HAND...'

And two more comments on the Korean plane, one equivocal . . .

. . . the other unequivocal.

Congress discovers that the president uses a hearing aid.

At last, James Watt does it to himself.

September 23, 1983

'THAT'S WHAT WE COULD DO — CHECK THEIR BLOODY KEEL FOR STEROIDS!'

WONDERS OF DEREGULATION— THE TWO-DOLLAR TRANSCONTINENTAL FLIGHT.

October 3, 1983

A presidential trip to the Philippines was planned then canceled.

October 6, 1983

The last . . .

. . . of James Watt.

October 21, 1983

'QUESTION: "AS A FEDERAL EMPLOYEE, ARE YOU IN FAVOR OF A NATIONAL HOLIDAY OBSERVING MARTIN LUTHER KING'S BIRTHDAY, OR DO YOU NOT PARTICULARLY CARE WHOSE BIRTHDAY IT IS?" ANSWER YES OR NO'

October 13, 1983

'GENERAL JARUZELSKI, SIR, IF THE NOBEL COMMITTEE HASN'T CALLED BY NOW TO ADMIT IT WAS ONLY A PRANK, THEY PROBABLY AREN'T GOING TO CALL!'

Lech Walesa wins the Nobel Peace Prize.

Watt moves out and the damn bears move right back in. But we got a new sheriff all nominated an' ready to go!

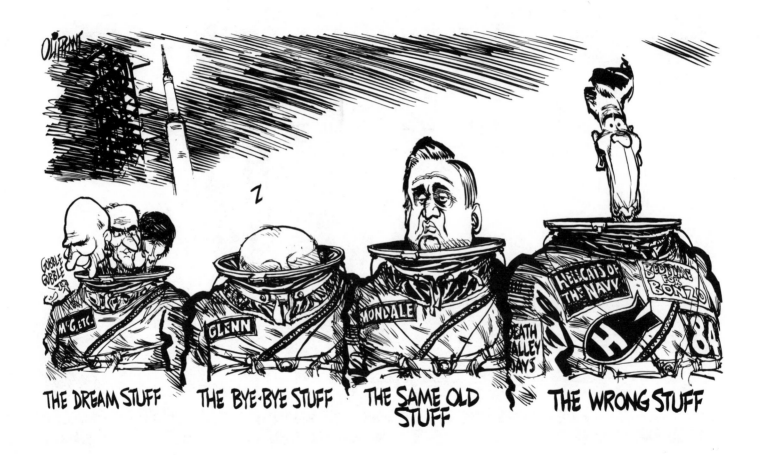

Jeane teases like a Doberman.

October 19, 1983

'THIS HERE'S JESSE AGAIN — WHAT Y'ALL GOT ON A COUPLE COMMERNISTS NAMED KENNEDY AND MOYNIHAN?'

A SORT OF IRISH SACCO AND VANZETTI!

Jesse Helms claimed to have an FBI file proving Martin Luther King was a communist, and that ain't all! So how can we possibly have a King national holiday?

'HEY, I'M SELLIN' A **DREAM** HERE! GEORGE WASHINGTON, OLD GLORY, THE CONSTITUTION, THE BILL OF RIGHTS, SEA-TO-SHININ'-SEA — WHAT'S NOT HAVIN' ENOUGH TO EAT GOT TO DO WITH IT?'

October 25, 1983

'WE HEAR YOUR SON MAY BE A CASUALTY IN THE BEIRUT BOMBING. GIVE US SOME COLOR ON THAT— LIKE ANGUISH, GRIEF, HOW YOU FEEL ABOUT IT...'

The marines are hit in Beirut. Back on the home front . . .

Grenada, that's where.

Press coverage of the Grenada invasion is tightly controlled.

The Grenada operation is a complete success.

In life, as on the stage, timing is everything.

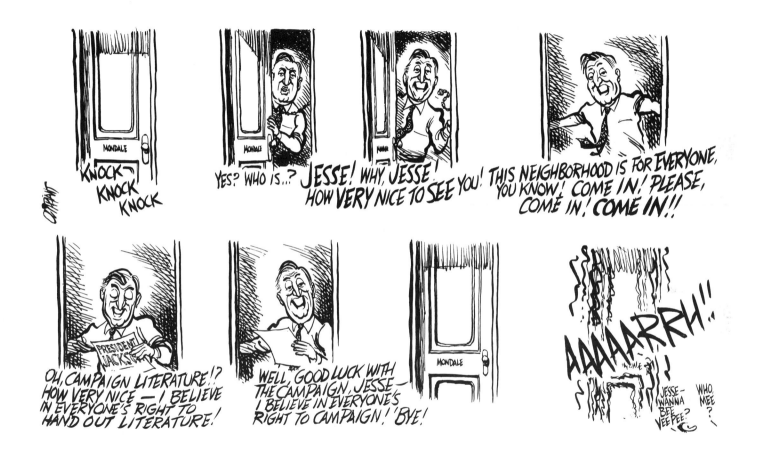

'THEY SAY IT'S HARD BEING PRESIDENT, BUT I SAY BEING A SPINELESS DEMOCRAT ON A FACT-FINDING TOUR, AIN'T EXACTLY A PICNIC!'

Ferreting out the truth about El Salvador, Honduras, Nicaragua, Grenada . . .

George breaks a tie . . .

The Wandering Palestinian.

November 15, 1983

'LESSEE... ONE BEIRUT SURPRISE, ONE GRENADA WHOOPEE, ONE NICARAGUA NIGHTMARE, ONE SUFFERIN' SALVADOR AND ONE BOTTLE OF SOLE SOURCE — AND THEY SAID IT GOES ON YOUR TAB.'

82

Where else?

Well, our invitation probably got lost in the mail. Or something.

But we thought she was only a little bit pregnant. . . .

November 29, 1983

At the Arms Control Talks, the Soviets step out for a while . . . for a while . . .

THE CABBAGE PATCH KID

Feldstein, the president's in-house critic. Feldstein, soon to become a household word . . . like Cabbage Patch doll!

December 2, 1983

No one has seen Soviet leader Yuri Andropov for weeks. . . .

'MERRY (WHOOPS) CHRISTMAS!'

Oh, well, they wouldn't have voted Republican anyway . . .

December 13, 1983

IF YOUNG EINSTEIN HAD GROWN UP IN THE U.S. EDUCATION SYSTEM ...

Still no Yuri Andropov.

December 28, 1983

AND NOW...THE MOVIE!

A Mr. Ray Bradbury wrote to the *Los Angeles Herald Examiner* calling this a "dumb" cartoon. One wonders if he'll find it dumb after four more years of Ronald Reagan. Better stay with science fiction. . . .

'I'VE DECIDED NOT TO PUNISH YOUR SUPERIOR OFFICERS — THEY'VE SUFFERED SO MUCH ALREADY!'

After the marine Beirut debacle.

Jesse Jackson gets a downed American flier back from Syria. And Martin Feldstein is still bugging Ronald Reagan.

January 6, 1984

'UM..DEAR? IT'S THE NEW TELEPHONE COMPANY REPAIR PERSON, AND, UM, IT'S NOT DEAR OLD MRS. BELL, AND, UM, IT LOOKS LIKE IT'S GOING TO BE EXPENSIVE.'

Ahem.

101

Charles Wick has reportedly been recording phone conversations at USIA. Just routine.

'ER, DER REPORT, SIR... VID MY APOLOGIES!'

It was the rest of the committee. *They* were the ones who left in all the nasty stuff, sir. . . .

Reagan receives the ambassador from the Vatican. And all this time we thought churches had something to do with religion.

Ethylene-dibromide. A preservative used in all sorts of foods.

'..THEN, WHEN I KISS YOU, OLGA, YOU TURN FROM AN UGLY OLD TOAD INTO A NOT-TOO-BAD-LOOKING BROAD, AND WE LIVE MORE-OR-LESS HAPPILY EVER AFTER.'

Listen to him. He's the actor.

'OH, GO AHEAD AND TAPE THE CRUD — AT LEAST WE'LL KNOW WE'RE DRIVING JACK VALENTI CRAZY.'

GLIMMERS OF AMIABILITY AS GROMYKO AND SHULTZ MEET IN PRIVATE.

'GRILLING THE CANDIDATES TODAY WILL BE EMILY BINKS-MUDDLE AS TED KOPPEL, AND CYNTHIA SNAPLEY AS PHIL DONAHUE.'

Can the League's debate death-grip be broken?

January 23, 1984

'THAT'S NOT HOW LIFE WORKS, MR. JACKSON — YOU CAN'T THROW ME OUT OF MY JOB SIMPLY TO SATISFY SOME RIDICULOUS QUOTA SYSTEM!'

Well, we're over-subscribed with Reagans . . .

CONFIRMATION HEARINGS: THE CONGRESSIONAL PUSSYCATS Vs. THE BIG MEESE.

Presidential buddy, Ed Meese, applies for attorney general. Let the hearings commence. . . .

January 25, 1984

You can't please everyone.

SCORNFUL OF THE DEFICIT DANGERS, HE SENT HIS MARINES TO DIE IN FAR-OFF LANDS FOR APPLE PIE, FOR CHURCH AND FLAG, FOR SCHOOL PRAYER, FOR HIS POLITICAL KEISTER.

SUDDENLY AMERICA WAS **STANDING TALL** (PG) . . . AND COST WAS NO OBSTACLE!

 DR ANDROPOV, OF THE EVIL EMPIRE. WHERE WAS HE?

 THE PHANTOM HUNGRY—THEY THREATENED A NATION WITH THEIR GREED.

 MOM. SHE WANTED SECURITY IN HER OLD AGE—BUT IT WAS A TOUGH WORLD OUT THERE.

 NERVOUS NELLIE. SHE FEARED THE BOMB. BUT NATIONS AREN'T BUILT BY SISSIES.

COSTARRING THE U.S. MARINES THE THE POPE GRENADA EURAC. EHHH! (CRUNCH) IT'S ONLY A MOVIE, DOC!

'HEY, LOOK, WE'RE WARM, WE'RE DRY, WE HAVE A ROOF OVER OUR HEADS, ENOUGH TO EAT...
SO WILL YOU QUIT WORRYING ABOUT THINGS WE CAN'T SEE.'

SO, RUN! SEE IF WE CARE! HA! WE'RE GLAD YOU'RE RUNNING!! IT'S JUST WHAT WE HOPED FOR! NOW YOU'RE IN REAL TROUBLE — BIG, BIG TROUBLE! YOU HEAR THAT? NOW WE CAN MAKE A RACE OF IT! HA!

IT'S A LONELY JOB, BUT SOME BODY HAS TO DO IT!

115

Reagan announces he will, indeed, run for a second term.

January 31, 1984

'I'M SORRY, BUT THE PRESIDENT CAN'T MEET WITH YOU NOW—HE HAS SOME HIGHER PRIORITIES TO ATTEND TO, LIKE ABORTION AND SCHOOL PRAYER.'

116

First things first.

OCCUPANT,
AFRICA.
WE ARE HAPPY TO ADVISE YOU THAT A DONATION
HAS BEEN MADE IN YOUR NAME TO THE
JESSE JACKSON FOR PRESIDENT CAMPAIGN.
SINCERELY, THE ARAB LEAGUE.

A great drought in starving Africa. And their neighbors have money to waste.

'TO CHOICE!'

Business as usual in Beirut.

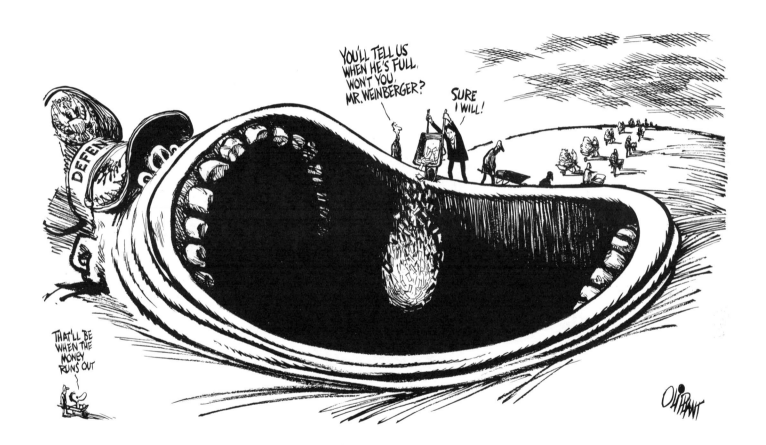

THERE HE GOES AGAIN.

Twinkletoes Reagan steps out of Beirut, but leaves a couple of warships to shell hell out of the place . . .

. . . which brings us back to Mr. Feldstein.

MUSICAL CHAIR

Yuri Andropov has died.

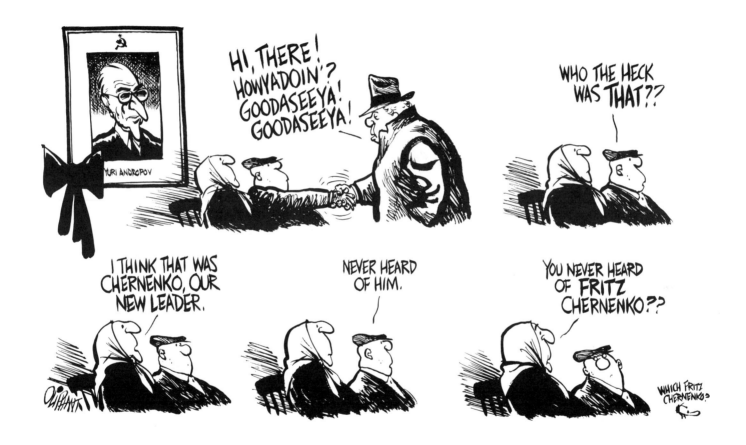

Let's get this country moving again.

'OH, STAND BACK, YOU BUNCH OF SILLIES—! 'LL GO CLAIM THE REWARD,, AND WE'LL **ALL** GO TO THE WHITE HOUSE!'

The "Hymie" incident.

Unions show their weight.

'YOU'RE GETTIN' THAT TROUBLE IN YOUR FUEL PUMP AGAIN.'

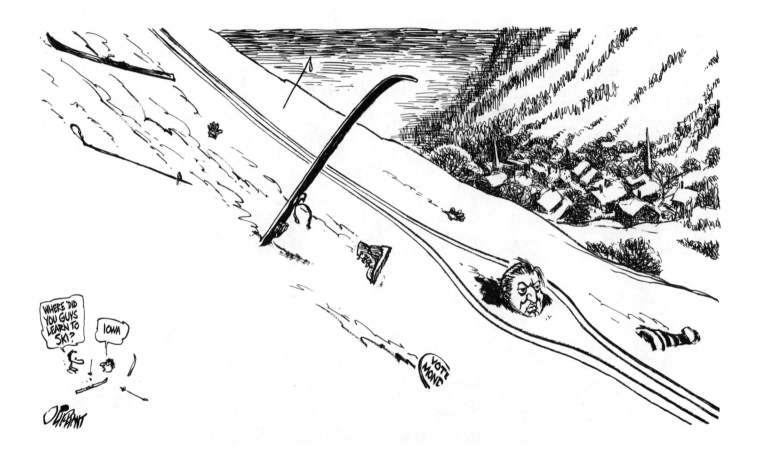

Gary Hart (soon to be Hartpence) wins over Mondale in New Hampshire.

'IF WE OFFERED HIM LOWER INTEREST RATES, MAYBE HE COULD BUY A TRACTOR.'

Prayer in the schools. Prayer in the schools. Will they ever stop?

Probably not.

March 5, 1984

Gary Hart's family name was once Hartpence. Somewhere along the way he changed it for reasons of his own. . . .

March 5, 1984

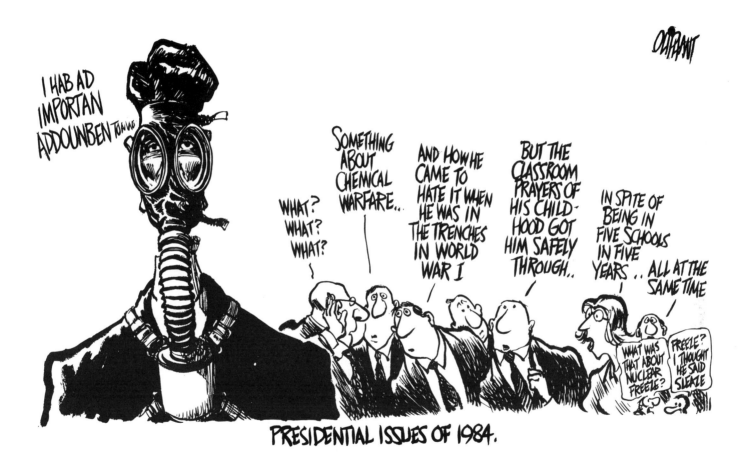

PRESIDENTIAL ISSUES OF 1984.

139

The president wants to resume the manufacture of chemical weapons. He also has begun a strange habit of relating stories about himself and others which never happened. . . .

The piety binge.

March 8, 1984

142

Forgiven mortgages. White House favors . . . the committee examining Meese for attorney general finds interesting anomalies.

'WHAT HAVE YOU DRAGGED IN **NOW??**'

Lord save us, it's the Killer Rabbit.

YUMPIES — Young Upwardly Mobile Professionals. Who thinks up these things?

'AH, YES... NATURE IS BEAUTIFUL IN HER OWN SAVAGE WAY.'

145

Oil company devouring oil company. No encouragement of exploration . . . just bite, chomp, swallow.

March 15, 1984

'HEY! HOWJA LIKE TO BE MY DEPUTY ASSISTANT ATTORNEY GENERAL?'

We know you and your favors — we'll probably end up in front of some House investigating committee . . .

'MR. FARRAKHAN'S FRIEND CLAIMS HE COULD TAKE OVER OUR RAINBOW COALITION AND REALLY WHIP IT INTO SOMETHING!'

Jesse Jackson refuses to renounce his close connection with a black racist named Farrakhan who called Hitler a "great man."

Elections in El Salvador.

'WE BELIEVE THE LIL' FELLAS LONG FOR A CHANCE TO EXPERIENCE DEMOCRACY AND THE ELECTORAL PROCESS AS WE KNOW IT.'

WHERE SHOULD OUR ISRAEL EMBASSY BE? OR: IN HOT PURSUIT OF THE JEWISH VOTE.

'YELL THAT ONE MORE TIME, I DARE YOU.'

"That lady" became famous for her "Where's the beef?" TV commercial. Walter Mondale became almost as famous by picking the term up and using it. It got rather old rather quickly.

TOXIC WASTE

Ah, Easter!

A Democratic house divided.

Anyone for Chinese food? The president goes to China.

ANSEL ADAMS
1902-1984

TWO WESTERNERS (CORRECT SCALE)

Overzealous political action groups keep collecting money, money, money for Walter Mondale, the special-interest candidate.

April 27, 1984

159

The China visit.

The Chinese televised Reagan's speech but offered no translation.

Black racist Farrakhan, a close friend of Jesse Jackson, threatened with death a black newspaperman who reported Jackson's "Hymie" remark. Jackson, a minister, proved a master of obfuscation.

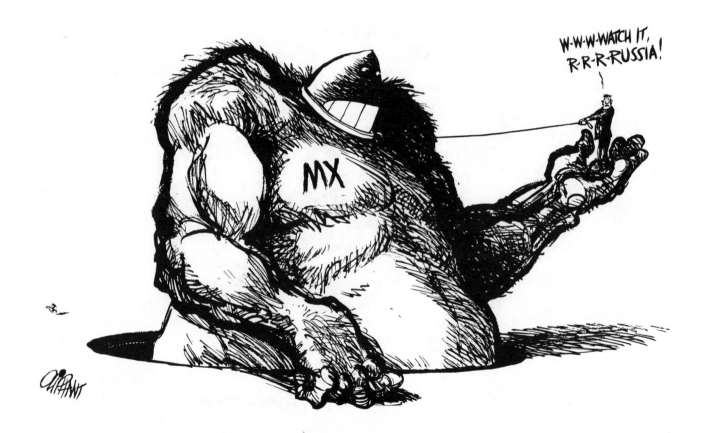

'CONGRATULATIONS! YOUR DEMOCRATIC ELECTIONS QUALIFY YOU FOR CERTAIN PRIVILEGES...'

HIS WORK COMPLETED, DR. FELDSTEIN LEAVES THE JUNGLE.

FEAR OF LIGHT.

Nobel Peace Prize winner Andrei Sakharov and his wife go on a hunger strike.
She was seeking medical attention outside the USSR. This was disallowed.

'C'MON, SAM, I PROMISE I'VE ALMOST GOT THE PROBLEM LICKED — JUST GIMME ONE MORE LITTLE DRINK TO KEEP ME GOING WHILE I FINISH HIM OFF!'

President Duarte visits Washington to convince Congress of his urgent needs, like more money.

'RELAX, COMRADE SAKHAROV — YOU ARE BEING PROVIDED WITH QUALIFIED MEDICAL AID.'

170

So says an official announcement by Soviet authorities.

'EVERYTHING LOOKS NICE AND NEAT FOR NOVEMBER, BOSS — EXCEPT FOR CASEY, OF COURSE...'

The briefing book caper is traced to CIA Director Casey.

'WE WRITE NO LAST CHAPTERS...' Reagan, Memorial Day, 1984.

At last, the Tomb of the Unknown Serviceman of the Vietnam War is dedicated.

Mondale believes he has it sewn up. Neither Hart nor Jackson accepts this.

For D-Day 40th Anniversary, June 6, 1984.

Much jubilation as the Reagans visit the Old Sod.